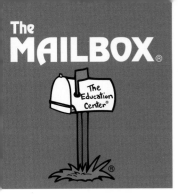

The MAILBOX®
The Education Center®

grades K-1

W9-AZY-137

Organize MAY Now!™

Everything You Need for a Successful May

Monthly Organizing Tools
Manage your time, classroom, and students with monthly organizational tools.

Essential Skills Practice
Practice essential skills this month with engaging activities and reproducibles.

May in the Classroom
Carry your monthly themes into every corner of the classroom.

Ready-to-Go Learning Centers and Skills Practice
Bring May to life right now!

Managing Editor: Sharon Murphy

Editorial Team: Becky S. Andrews, Kimberley Bruck, Karen P. Shelton, Diane Badden, Thad H. McLaurin, Kimberly Brugger-Murphy, Cindy K. Daoust, Lynn Drolet, Gerri Primak, Kelly Robertson, Allison E. Ward, Karen A. Brudnak, Hope Rodgers, Dorothy C. McKinney, Janet Boyce, Catherine Broome-Kehm, Rebecca Brudwick, Norma Cooper, Jill Davis, Stacie Stone Davis, Margaret Elliott, Cathy Gerik, Ada Goren, Michelle M. Jenkins, Angie Kutzer, Beth Marquardt, Margie McGreevy, Valerie Wood Smith, Angela Falter Thomas, Susan Walker

Production Team: Lisa K. Pitts, Pam Crane, Rebecca Saunders, Jennifer Tipton Cappoen, Chris Curry, Sarah Foreman, Theresa Lewis Goode, Clint Moore, Greg D. Rieves, Barry Slate, Donna K. Teal, Zane Williard, Tazmen Carlisle, Marsha Heim, Lynette Dickerson, Mark Rainey, Angela Kamstra, Sheila Krill

www.themailbox.com

Table of Contents

Monthly Organizing Tools
A collection of reproducible forms, notes, and other timesavers and organizational tools just for May.

Essential Skills Practice
Fun, skill-building activities and reproducibles that combine the skills your students must learn with favorite May themes.

May in the Classroom
In a hurry to find a specific type of May activity? It's right here!

Ready-to-Go Learning Centers and Skills Practice
Two center activities you can tear out and use almost instantly! Plus a collection of additional reproducible skill builders!

Skills Grid

	Cinco de Mayo	Flowers	Bees	Mother's Day	End of Year	Centers	Games	Time Fillers	Writing Ideas & Prompts	Learning Center: A Box of Blooms	Learning Center: Biscuits and Honey	Ready-to-Go Skills Practice
Literacy												
ABC order					49							
beginning sounds			32									
initial consonants: *b, t*												90
consonant blends			35									
word families: *-in, -ip*		29										
long-vowel word families: *-ice, -ide*												92
r-controlled vowel: *ar*		30										
onsets and rimes						58						
recognizing words	18											
rhyming words										89		
sight words		22										
high-frequency words			34									
compound words			37									
contractions												93
spelling								68				
parts of speech		24										
journal prompts									70			
prewriting									71			
writing		23	33	40	44				70, 71			
friendly letter					46							
ending punctuation						59					74, 81	
editing								69				
critical thinking								68				
skill review					45		62					
following directions	19											
following oral directions							63					
Math												
number recognition		22										
comparing sets							62					
skip-counting			33									
commutative property of addition		24										
addition facts to 8			38									
addition to 18 with three addends			39									
addition word problems to 10											82, 89	
addition word problems to 18											82	
subtraction facts to 10		23										
addition and subtraction						59						
addition and subtraction to 18												96
word problems												95
fact families		34										
place value	21											
fractions	20											
fractions: parts of a group							63					
nonstandard measurement												94
estimating weight	18											
ordering days of the week												91
calendar			32									
understanding time					46							
modeling money amounts		25										
coin recognition					45							
graphing				42								
patterns						58						
skill review					44							
Science												
life cycle of a flower		25										
parts of a bee			35									
Creative Arts												
making a card				40								

Medallion

Tape to a student's clothing or glue to a crepe paper necklace.

Brag Tag

Use a child's words to finish the sentence starter.

©The Mailbox® • *Organize May Now!*™ • TEC60983

Award

_____
student

is "bee-ing" noticed for:

_____   _____
teacher   date

©The Mailbox® • *Organize May Now!*™ • TEC60983

Medallion, brag tag, and award: Copy onto colorful construction paper, cut out, and use as desired.

May

Sunday	Monday	Tuesday	Wednesday	Thursday	Friday	Saturday

Center Checklist

Center

Name

Class List

Name																

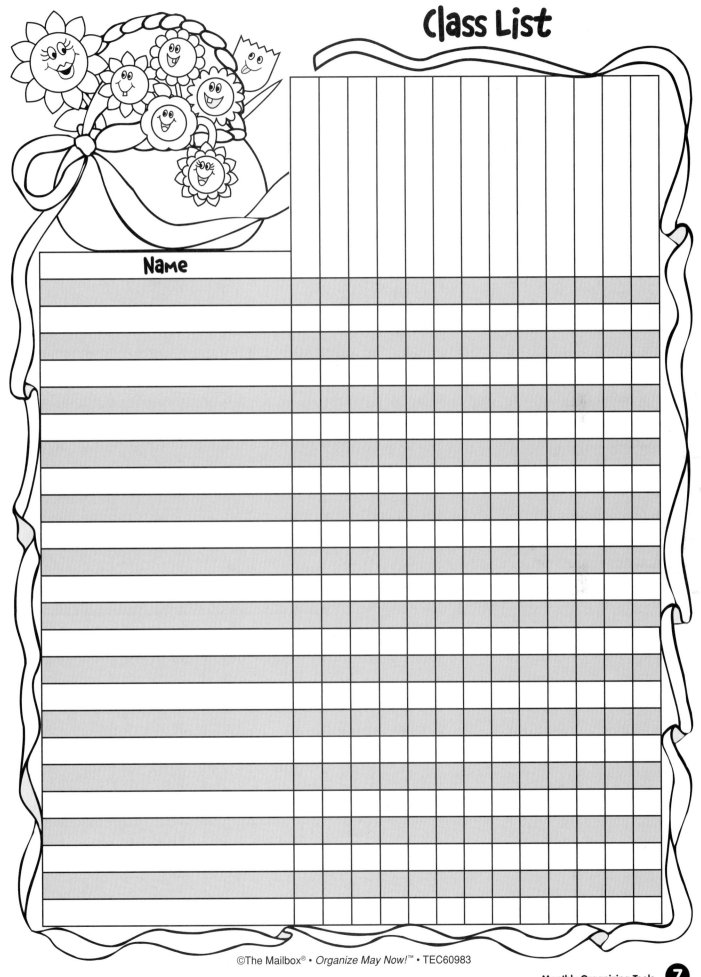

Classroom News

From _____

Date _____

Help Wanted

Special Thanks

Look What We Are Learning

Superstars

Please Remember

Classroom News

From _____

Date _____

9

WHAT'S THE BUZZ?

TEC60983

TEC60983

TEC60983

TEC60983

Cinco de Mayo!

TEC60983

Clip art: Use the artwork on student papers and on correspondence such as announcements, forms, and parent notes.

Name _____

Goal _____

I'm "berry" proud of you!

You're a star!

Name _____

Goal _____

Name _____

Goal _____

_____

Keep trying!

Incentive charts: Have students track their progress as they work toward a variety of goals.

Monthly Organizing Tools ⑪

My Journal

Name

Journal cover: Make this page the front cover of your students' writing journals.

Meetings:

Birthdays & Special Dates:

Duties This Month:

Themes:

Materials to Collect:

To Do:

Monthly planning form: Use this handy form to stay on top of May's school-related responsibilities.

Open: Use this page for parent correspondence, or use it with students too. For example, ask each child to write (or dictate as you write) a story about a giant berry, words that rhyme with *berry,* or math story problems about berries.

Parent reminder note: Use this note to remind parents of supply requests, field trips, and special events such as a classroom party, a school program, or a guest speaker.

School Note

©The Mailbox® • *Organize May Now!™* • TEC60983

SCHOOL NOTE

©The Mailbox® • *Organize May Now!™* • TEC60983

School notes: Use these notes for parent communications such as announcing an upcoming event, requesting supplies or volunteers, and writing messages of praise.

Family Fun

You'll plant memories and watch your child's confidence grow as you share in decorating this special project. Work with your child to decorate the flowerpot. Use whatever supplies you have on hand, such as scraps of paper, foil, gift wrap, or fabric.

We hope to see your completed project by _____.

Sincerely,

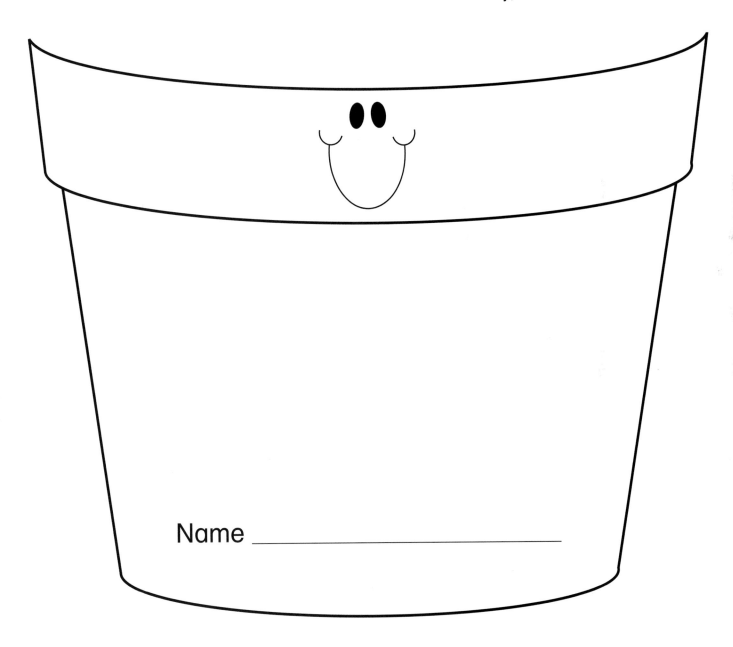

Name _____

Learning Links: fine-motor skills, creativity

Note to the teacher: Date and sign a copy of the page. Make student copies on construction paper; then write each child's name on the pot before sending it home with her. When a child returns her project and shares it with the class, help her make a tissue paper flower. Post the flower and the pot on a display titled "Family Flowerpots."

Cinco de Mayo

Olé! Celebrate Cinco de Mayo on May 5. The festive holiday commemorates a major battle fought in 1862 for Mexico's independence.

Literacy

Recognizing words

said

said

Cakewalk!

Cakewalk!

Invite students to take part in this sweet variation of a popular Cinco de Mayo tradition. For each child, program an index card with a familiar word. Copy each word onto a separate paper slip, fold it, and then drop it into a container. In a large open area, arrange the cards in a circle. Have each child stand behind a different card. Play some lively Mexican music as each youngster walks from card to card. When the music stops, each student stops and silently reads the closest card. Draw a slip from the container and announce the word. The student who is closest to the matching card announces, "Cakewalk!" After several rounds, make everyone a winner by giving each child a cupcake.

Math

Estimating weight

Piñata Practice

Piñatas are a part of many fiestas, and Cinco de Mayo is no exception. In advance, secretly place a different amount of wrapped candies in a paper cup for each small group of students. Tape a second cup over the first to make a piñata base as shown. To make a piñata, give each small group a prepared base. Invite the groups to decorate the piñatas by gluing on pieces of colorful tissue paper. When the piñatas are dry, place them at a center. A child estimates the weight of each piñata and then places them in order from lightest to heaviest. To check his work, he weighs each pinata on a balance scale and adjusts the placement as needed.

Find reproducible activities on pages 19–21.

Hat Dance

Name _____

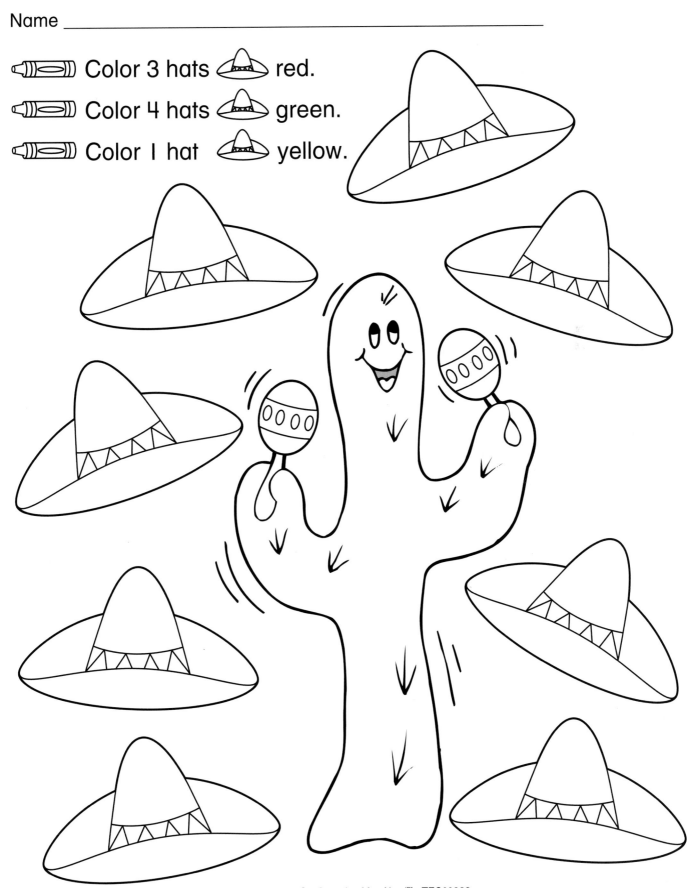

Color 3 hats red.

Color 4 hats green.

Color 1 hat yellow.

Following Directions 19

Fraction Fiesta

Name _____

Color each item that shows equal parts.

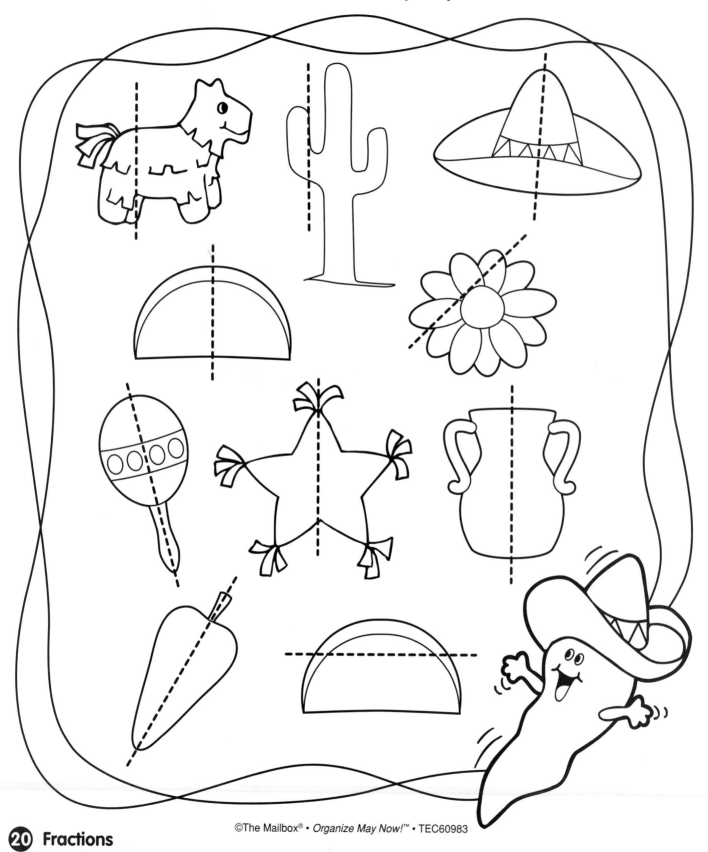

Olé!

Name _____

Read each clue. 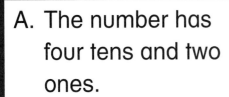 Write the number.

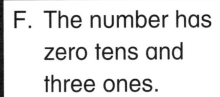 Color the matching pepper.

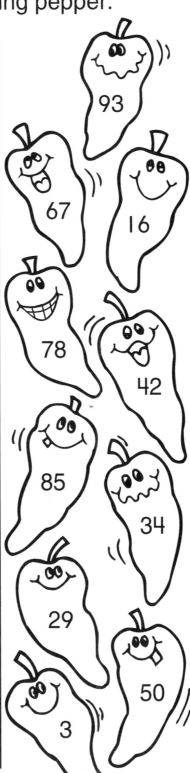

A. The number has four tens and two ones.

_____

B. The number has six tens and seven ones.

_____

C. The number has nine tens and three ones.

_____

D. The number has two tens and nine ones.

_____

E. The number has eight tens and five ones.

_____

F. The number has zero tens and three ones.

_____

G. The number has one ten and six ones.

_____

H. The number has three tens and four ones.

_____

I. The number has five tens and zero ones.

_____

J. The number has seven tens and eight ones.

_____

Flowers

• *Sight words*

like

with

Flower Freeze

To prepare for this whole-group game, cut out several extra large flower shapes from bulletin board paper and label each one with a different sight word. Spread out the flowers on the floor in an open area of the classroom. On your signal, students walk in the same direction from flower to flower with their arms out to resemble flying butterflies. When you say "freeze," youngsters stop walking. In turn, each child reads aloud the word on the flower closest to him. Then continue the game in the same manner as time allows.

Number recognition • • • • • • • • • • • • • • • • • • • Math

Blooming Numbers

This hundred chart activity provides a bunch of number practice. Prepare a class supply of construction paper flower cutouts (use the small flower patterns on page 26 if desired). Cut a hole in the center of each flower so that only one number can be seen through the flower when placed on a hundred chart. Give each child a prepared flower cutout and a hundred chart. Announce a number. Then direct each youngster to locate the number on her chart and position her flower so that the number shows through the center. Scan for accuracy and then continue in the same manner for a desired number of rounds. For more advanced students, announce a number in tens and ones for them to locate on their charts.

1	2	3	4	5	6	7	8	9	10
11	12	13	14	15	16	17	18	19	20
21	23	24	25	26	27	28	29	30
	32		34	35	36	37	38	39	40
41	43	44	45	46	47	48	49	50
51	52	53	54	55	56	57	58	59	60
61	62	63	64	65	66	67	68	69	70
71	72	73	74	75	76	77	78	79	80
81	82	83	84	85	86	87	88	89	90
91	92	93	94	95	96	97	98	99	100

Cultivate your growing learners with this blooming collection of ideas!

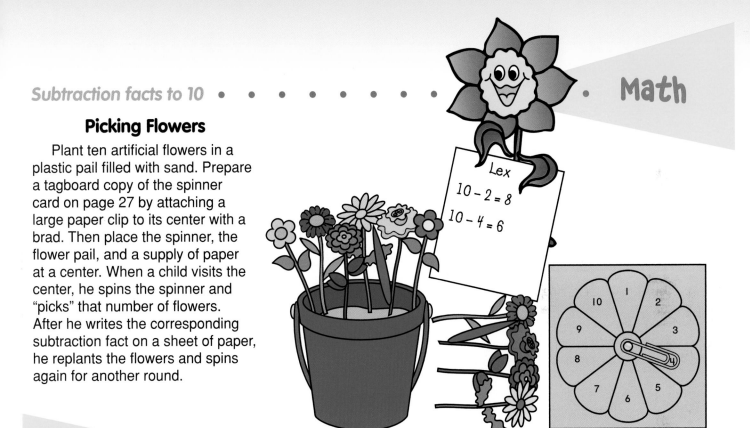

Math

Subtraction facts to 10 • • • • • • • • • • • •

Picking Flowers

Plant ten artificial flowers in a plastic pail filled with sand. Prepare a tagboard copy of the spinner card on page 27 by attaching a large paper clip to its center with a brad. Then place the spinner, the flower pail, and a supply of paper at a center. When a child visits the center, he spins the spinner and "picks" that number of flowers. After he writes the corresponding subtraction fact on a sheet of paper, he replants the flowers and spins again for another round.

Lex
10 – 2 = 8
10 – 4 = 6

Literacy • Writing

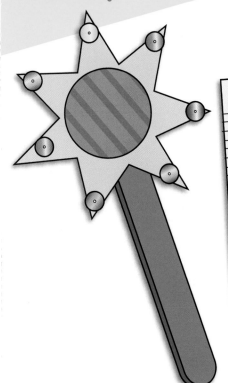

Sydney

My flower is a sunrose. It likes sunny places. It smells like a rose. It needs some perfume every day.

What Pretty Flowers!

Spark youngsters' imaginations with this nifty project! Set out chosen arts-and-crafts materials, such as construction paper, craft sticks, pompoms, and wallpaper or gift wrap scraps. A child uses the materials to create a new type of flower. Then, on a sheet of paper, she writes about her flower, including its name, where it grows, and its needs. Display each child's flower and completed paper together on a board or tabletop along with a title such as "[Teacher's name] Flower Shop." As students have time to spare, invite them to browse the flower shop.

Adjectives	Nouns	Verbs
red	flowers	grow
pink	pots	fall
tiny	seeds	sprout
little	dirt	pick
pretty	garden	plant

dirt

pick

little

red

flowers

plant

Liz

Tiny seeds grow into flowers.

I plant flowers in red pots.

Sprouting Sentences

To prepare for this center, use the small flower patterns on page 26 to make a supply of flower cutouts in three different colors. Program one set of flowers with adjectives, one set with nouns, and the third set with verbs (see the suggestions). Store each set of flowers in a separate container. Place the containers and a supply of writing paper at a center. When a child visits the center, she removes one flower from each container. Then she uses the words to form a complete sentence and writes it on a sheet of paper. After she returns the flowers to their containers, she continues in the same manner as time allows.

Placing Petals

Make a simple workmat with two flowers like the ones shown (without petals). Also cut out nine petals from each of two colors of construction paper. Store the petals in a resealable plastic bag. Place the bag, the workmat, a set of cards numbered from 1 to 9, and a supply of paper at a center. A center visitor selects two number cards to represent two addends. He positions petals around the flowers to correspond with the addends. Then he records the math fact and its answer on a sheet of paper. Next, he switches the petals from one flower to the other to show the inverse of the fact and records the number sentence. He continues in the same manner as time allows.

Samuel

5 + 4 = 9

4 + 5 = 9

8 + 3 = 11

8

3

Modeling money amounts

"Cent-sational" Blooms

For each child in a small group, cut out and laminate a copy of the large flower pattern on page 26. Gather a group of students and give each child a flower, a wipe-off marker, and an assortment of imitation coins. Announce a cash amount that can be shown in various ways. Each youngster writes the amount in the center of her flower. Then she uses the coins to model the amount in different ways, displaying each set on a different flower petal. After each child counts her coins to verify her answers, she cleans off her flower to prepare for another round.

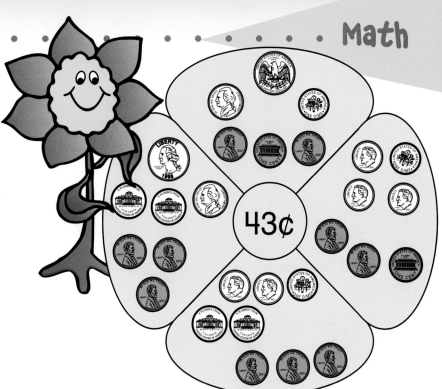

Science

Life cycle of a flower

A Seed Story

Youngsters explore how a seed changes to a flower with this booklet-making project! Give each child a construction paper copy of the booklet pages on page 28 and two 4" x 5" construction paper covers. Invite students to read the text aloud with you, stopping for discussion as desired. After having youngsters cut out the pages, guide them through the directions shown below to complete each page. When the pages are dry, help each student write a desired title on her cover, sign her name, and staple her pages in order between the covers. Encourage each youngster to read her book to a partner before taking it home to share with her family.

Page 1: Color the sky. Spread glue below the seed (not over the text) and sprinkle sand over the wet glue to resemble soil.
Page 2: Color the ground and the sun. Make blue fingerprint raindrops on the sky.
Page 3: Color the ground and the sun. Glue small pieces of yarn below the seed to resemble roots.
Page 4: Color the ground and the plant's stem and leaves. Glue small pieces of balled up tissue paper to make a flower.

Find reproducible activities on pages 29–31.

Small Flower Patterns

Use with "Blooming Numbers" on page 22 and "Sprouting Sentences" on page 24.

TEC60983

TEC60983

Large Flower Pattern

Use with "'Cent-sational' Blooms" on page 25.

TEC60983

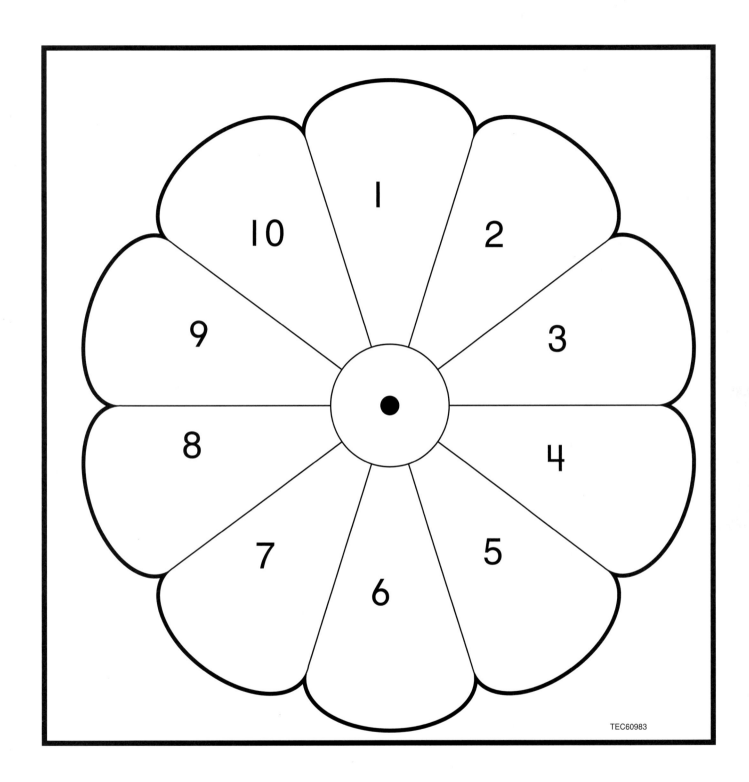

TEC60983

The seed needs water, light, and air.

2

Then a stem, leaves, and a flower grow!

4

Plant a seed in the soil.

1

Roots grow down in the soil.

3

Pretty Pots

Cut.

Glue to match the word family.

-ip

-in

©The Mailbox® • Organize May Now!™ • TEC60983

Fresh-Cut Flowers

Name _____

Complete each sentence.
Use the word bank.

To
Mom

Word Bank

| hard | card | large | garden |
| part | far | park | star |

1. Flowers grow in the _____.

2. Planting a garden is _____ work.

3. A stem is _____ of a flower.

4. Ladybug likes to play at the _____.

5. The _____ is for her mom.

6. One flower is shaped like a _____.

7. The watering can is very _____.

8. Ladybug is _____ from the ground.

R-Controlled Vowel: ar   ©The Mailbox® • *Organize May Now!*™ • TEC60983

Blooming Flower

Color the flower. Glue a small photo of yourself to the center of the flower. On each leaf, write one way you have changed or one thing you have learned this year. Lightly color the leaves with a green crayon. Cut out the leaves and the flower; glue them to a paper stem.

Finished Project

Look How I've

Bloomed!

Bees

· · · · · · · · · · · · · ***Beginning sounds***

wings

Bee Buddies

To prepare for this honey-of-a-partner center, cut out two yellow construction paper copies of the bee pattern on page 56 and add desired details. Laminate the bees and tape on pipe cleaner antennae. For each letter you would like youngsters to review, cut out a set of wings from an overhead transparency similar to the one shown. Label each wing set with an uppercase and a lowercase letter. Place the wings, the bees, and two black wipe-off markers at a center.

When a twosome visits the center, each child places a set of wings above a bee. Then she writes (or draws) words on the bee that begin with the corresponding letter. Once both students are satisfied with their lists, they trade bees and read each other's responses. After wiping the bees clean, they each choose a different set of wings and continue in the same manner as time allows.

Calendar · · · · · · · · · · · · · · · · **Math**

It's a Date!

Sharpen students' calendar skills with a buzzing bee pointer! To make a bee pointer, cut out a yellow construction paper copy of one of the bee patterns on page 52. Tape the bee to a dowel rod or an unsharpened pencil. During calendar time, announce a calendar-related task, such as "point to the second Thursday in the month" or "point to the date that is two days after the 14th." Invite a child to buzz like a bee as she moves the pointer in a flying motion to the answer on the calendar. Continue in the same manner, inviting other students to use the pointer.

May 2006						
S	M	T	W	T	F	S
	1	2	3	4	5	6
7	8	9	10			13
14	15	16	17	18	19	
21	22	23	24	25	26	27
28	29	30	31			

"Bee-dazzle" your youngsters with this sweet collection of skill-based ideas!

Honeycomb Counting

To prepare for this center, label each of three plastic jars with a different skip-counting pattern: twos, fives, or tens. Place a supply of Honeycomb cereal in each jar, making sure the total amount of cereal pieces can be evenly counted using the corresponding number pattern. Program the bottom of each jar with its total amount for self-checking. Place the jars and a sheet of waxed paper at a center.

When a youngster visits the center, he pours the contents of one jar onto the waxed paper. Then he arranges the cereal pieces in groups to correspond with the labeled counting pattern. To determine the total amount, he counts the cereal as designated as he points to each corresponding set. After checking his answer, he returns the cereal to the jar and continues in the same manner for each remaining jar.

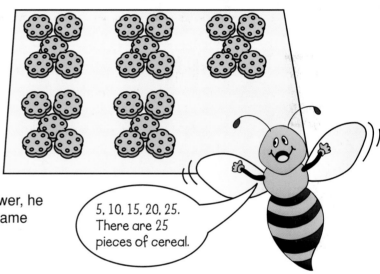

5, 10, 15, 20, 25. There are 25 pieces of cereal.

I help at home. I make my bed and clean my room. I also help Mom make dinner.
by Chloe

Busy as a Bee

Explain to students that worker bees have a variety of jobs, such as cleaning the hive and feeding others. Then invite youngsters to discuss some of the responsibilities they have at home. On a sheet of paper, have each child write about her jobs at home and make several yellow fingerprints around her writing. After the prints dry, direct her to use a fine-tip marker to transform the prints to smiling bees. Mount each completed paper on a slightly larger sheet of black construction paper, and display the projects along with the title "We're Busy Bees!"

A Full Hive

Youngsters bring honey to the hive with this lotto game! Make a copy of the beehive pattern on page 36 and divide it into seven sections as shown. Then make a copy of the prepared hive for each child. List 12 high-frequency words on the board. Have each child cut out his beehive and randomly program each section with a different word from the list. Also give each child seven pieces of Honeycomb or Honey Nut Cherrios cereal to use as counters.

To play, announce a word from the list. If a student has the word on his hive, he covers it with a cereal piece. The first child to cover all the words on his hive buzzes like a bee. After checking his words, continue the game until each child has covered all of his words.

Fact families · Math

Buzzing Around

To prepare for this small-group game, cut out four construction paper copies of the beehive pattern on page 36. Label each hive with three numbers of a different fact family. Post the hives on the board, leaving ample space for writing under each one. Invite four students to pretend they are bees, "fly" to the board, and each stand near a different hive. On your signal, have each bee write below the hive one fact from the corresponding fact family. Invite the seated students to check the facts and then have the bees buzz back to their seats. Continue in the same manner until each fact family is complete.

Build a Bee

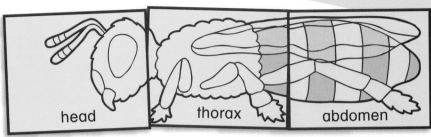

head   thorax   abdomen

This small-group game reinforces the fact that a bee's body is made up of three parts: the head, the thorax, and the abdomen. After sharing this information with students, have each child cut out a construction paper copy of the bee cards on page 36. Assign each student to a small group. Direct group members to mix their cards together and stack them facedown. To play, a child draws a card and announces the bee body part. Then she places the card faceup in front of her. Players take turns in the same manner until each player forms a bee. If a child draws a card that she already has, she returns it to the bottom of the stack.

Literacy • • • • • • • • • • • • • • **Consonant blends**

sl

bl   tr

fl   fr   pl

gr   cr   dr

fly

Toss Up

Phonics skills and motor skills take flight with this activity! Cut out a large hive shape from bulletin board paper. Divide it into sections and label them with different consonant blends. Place the cutout on the floor in an open area. To take a turn, a child stands a designated distance from the hive and tosses a beanbag on it. After she announces the blend that the beanbag is on, she names a word that begins with that blend. Then she buzzes as she picks up the beanbag, returns to the starting point, and gives the beanbag to the next student. If desired, chart students' responses to avoid repetition of words.

Find reproducible activities on pages 37–39.

Beehive Pattern

Use with "A Full Hive" and "Buzzing Around" on page 34.

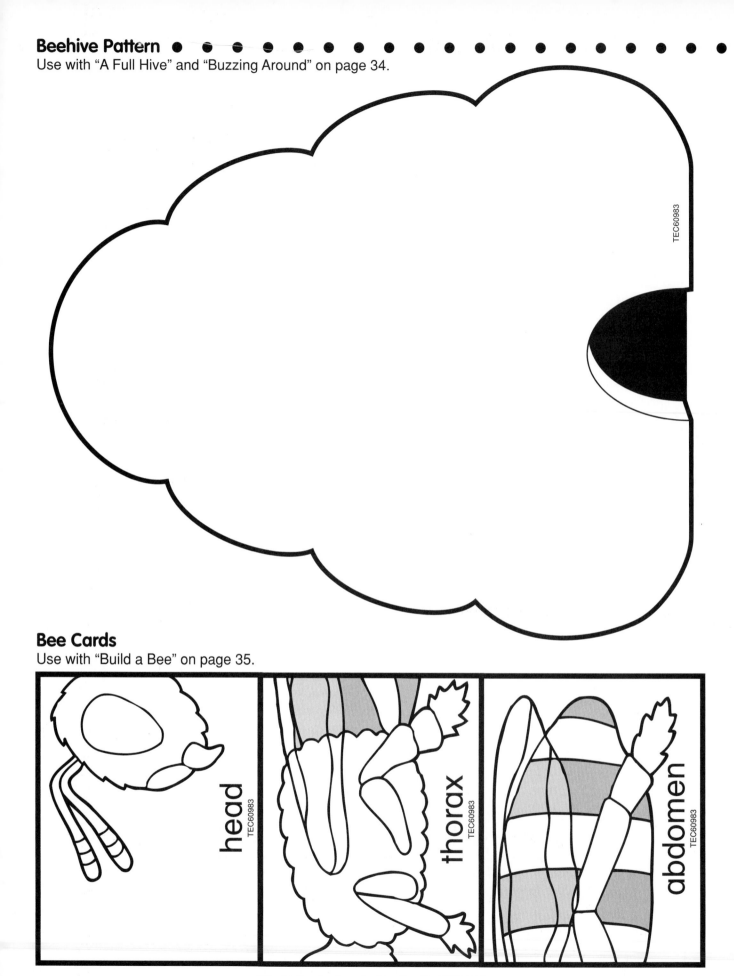

TEC60983

Bee Cards

Use with "Build a Bee" on page 35.

head   TEC60983

thorax   TEC60983

abdomen   TEC60983

Honey Makers

Name _____

Use the word bank to make each word a compound word.
Cut. Glue to match each picture to a word.

Word Bank

bug	fly	bow	bath
pot	shine	hive	brush

1. butter _____

2. rain _____

3. bird _____

4. lady _____

5. tooth _____

6. sun _____

7. flower _____

8. bee _____

Hive, Sweet Hive

Name _____

 Cut. Add.

Use the counters to help you.

3 + 3 = _____

6 + 1 = _____   5 + 2 = _____

2 + 3 = _____   3 + 5 = _____

4 + 1 = _____   4 + 3 = _____

6 + 2 = _____   4 + 2 = _____

4 + 4 = _____   7 + 1 = _____

Buzzing Home!

Add.

Help Mr. Bee get home.

If the answer is **12** or **14,** color the honeycomb cell **yellow.**

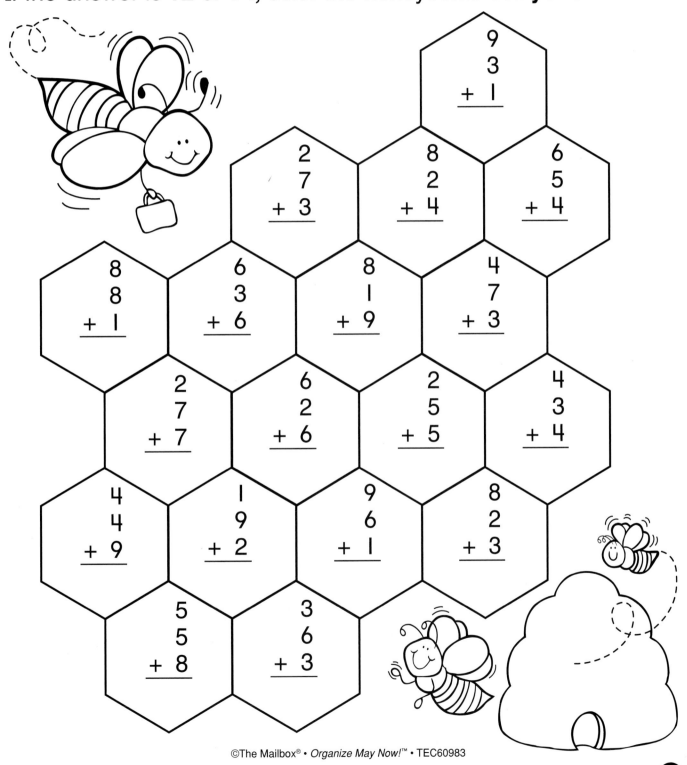

Mother's Day

It's easy for youngsters to express their appreciation for Mom with these thoughtful ideas.

Literacy

Writing

Mom's Favorites

This take-home survey encourages youngsters to compare their favorites with their moms' childhood favorites. Give each child a copy of page 41. Ask him to draw a picture of himself in the top box and then draw a picture of his mom in the lower box. Read aloud the sentence starters and have each child write to complete the sentences on the top section. Then ask him to take the survey home to complete the bottom sentences with his mom. When each child returns his survey, allow time for sharing with the class.

Making a card

Creative Arts

Petal Pickin'

This flower will be Mom's first pick when she's looking for a little help at home. Ask each youngster to write a different chore that she could do for her mom on each of five colorful construction paper flower petals. Have her glue a copy of her school photo on a construction paper circle. Then help her glue the petals on the back of the circle to make a flower. To complete the project, have her glue the flower on a sheet of construction paper and add desired details.

Find reproducible activities on pages 42–43.

Name _____

Me

1. My favorite toy is _____

   _____

2. My favorite game is _____

   _____

3. My favorite school subject is _____

   _____

My mom

1. My mom's favorite toy was _____

   _____

2. My mom's favorite game was _____

   _____

3. My mom's favorite school subject was _____

   _____

Note to the teacher: Use with "Mom's Favorites" on page 40.

Mother's Day 41

Great Gifts for Mom!

Name _____

🖐 2 3 4 5 Count. 🖍 Color the graph.

Mom's Gifts

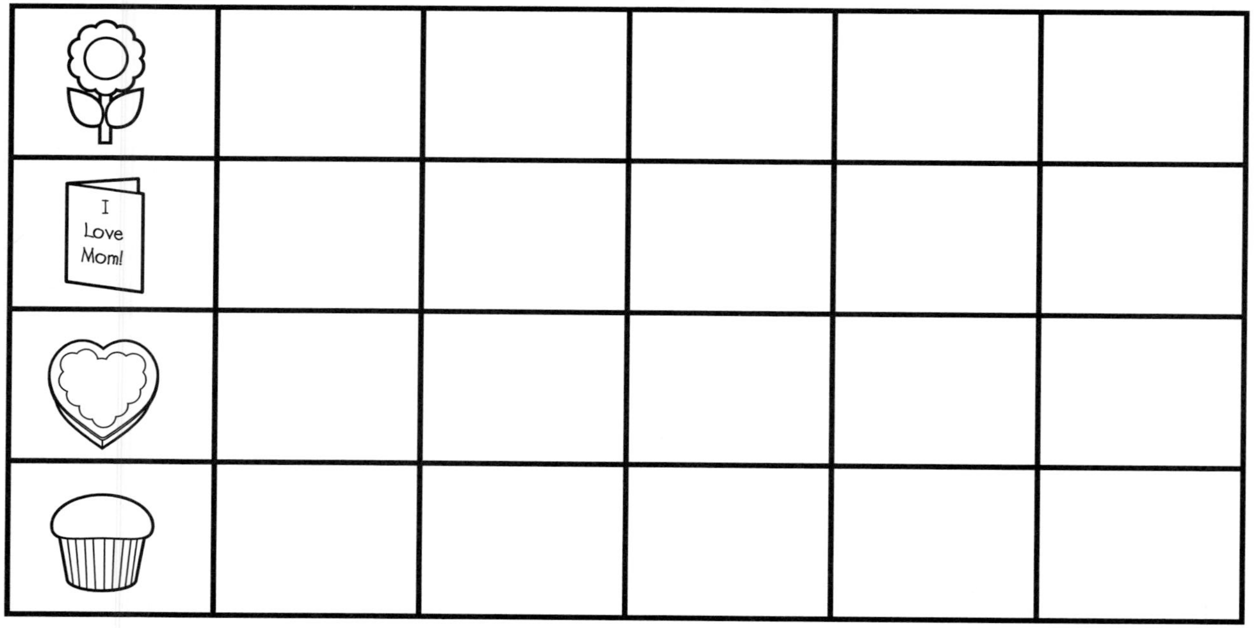

🌸					
I Love Mom!					
💗					
🧁					

✏️ Write.

How many more 💗 than 📄 ? _____

How many more 💗 than 🧁 ? _____

How many less 🧁 than 🌸 ? _____

✏️ Circle.

Which has more? 🧁 🌸

Which has more? 💗 📄

Which has less? 🌸 🧁

©The Mailbox® • *Organize May Now!*™ • TEC60983

Graphing

"Bee" Happy, Mom!

Use the patterns to create a "bee-autiful" card for Mother's Day! Personalize the wing. Color and cut out the patterns. Glue the wings on the bee. Add pipe cleaner antennae.

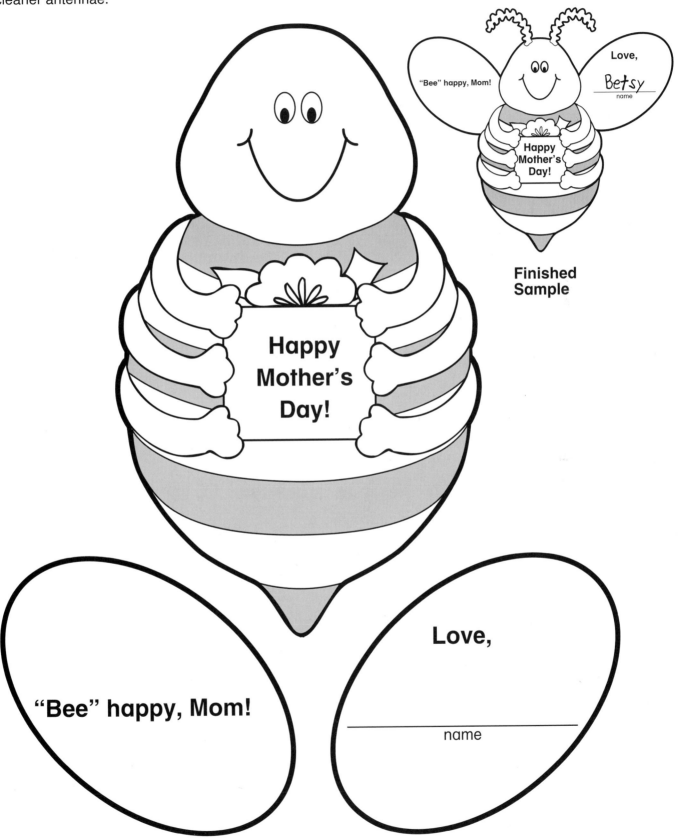

Quick Craft

Finished Sample

Happy Mother's Day!

"Bee" happy, Mom!

Love,

name

End of Year

Amy
I learned how to write sentences.

Year-End Reflections

This confidence-boosting display shows students how much they've learned this school year. To begin, have each child write (or dictate as you write) on an index card one thing she learned this year. Also direct her to draw a self-portrait on a sheet of white paper, trim around it, and glue it to an oval cut from aluminum foil to resemble a mirror. Invite youngsters to share their year-end reflections before mounting them on a board titled "Mirror, Mirror, on the Wall, We Have Learned a Lot Since the Fall!"

Skill review

Math

Each Day Counts

Count down the last days of school with this sunny activity! For each remaining day of school, program a 1" x 12" orange construction paper strip with a different math review activity. Form each strip into a loop with the writing inside. Staple the loops around a yellow construction paper circle to resemble a sun and its rays; then add desired details.

Each day, invite a child to choose a ray. Remove the ray and read the activity aloud for students to complete. After completing the last activity on the last day of school, comment on how many new math skills your youngsters have learned this year!

Write six addition problems with a sum of 6.

Draw and label a square, a rectangle, a triangle, and a circle.

Write ten numbers that are greater than 9.

Starting at 8, count by twos until 20.

Keep youngsters engaged during the final days of school with this sunny collection of skill-based ideas!

Super Sale

Not only is a class garage sale a great way to clean your classroom but it also provides youngsters with real-world math practice! To prepare, gather items from your classroom that you no longer need, such as class-made books, posters, charts, flash cards, puzzles, or extra books. Label each item with a price that corresponds to the value of one coin, varying the prices as desired. Display the items for easy student access. In a small bag, place an imitation coin or coin cutout to correspond with each labeled price. Have each child remove a coin, name it, and identify its value. Then invite each youngster to "buy" an item that has the same value as her coin.

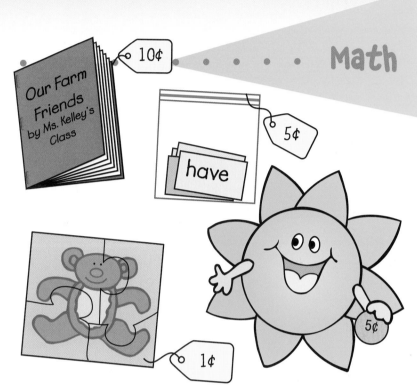

Pack Up!

Youngsters gear up for summertime travel with this sorting center. To prepare, trim a folded sheet of construction paper to resemble a suitcase, keeping the fold intact. Make one or more suitcases in the same manner. Select a grade-appropriate sorting skill—such as beginning sounds, vowels, word families, or syllables—and label the suitcases accordingly. Cut out a supply of the clothes patterns on page 47 and program each one to correspond with the chosen skill. Place the cutouts and suitcases at a center. When a child visits the center, he sorts each piece of clothing into the appropriate suitcase.

Literacy

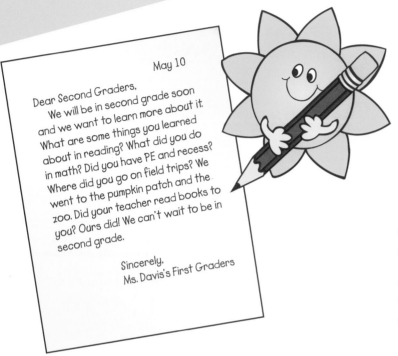

May 10

Dear Second Graders,
We will be in second grade soon and we want to learn more about it. What are some things you learned about in reading? What did you do in math? Did you have PE and recess? Where did you go on field trips? We went to the pumpkin patch and the zoo. Did your teacher read books to you? Ours did! We can't wait to be in second grade.

Sincerely,
Ms. Davis's First Graders

Sneak Preview

Team up with a teacher in the next grade level for this class activity. Encourage youngsters to think of questions they have about the upcoming grade level. On a sheet of chart paper, enlist students' help in writing a letter to the students in the next grade that incorporates some of their questions. Be sure to include all of the elements of a friendly letter (heading, greeting, body, closing, and signature). If desired, give youngsters a sneak preview of the next grade level by taking them with you to deliver the letter. After the other class replies, invite students to read aloud the letter to find out the answers to their questions. For more advanced students, arrange for each child to write his own letter to a student in the next grade.

Understanding time

Math

Sensational Summer Schedule

Invite youngsters to discuss what the morning, afternoon, and evening of a perfect summer day would include. Then help each child position a sheet of paper vertically, fold it into thirds as shown, and draw lines over the creases. In the top section of his paper, have him write a time that corresponds to the morning and then draw a picture of an activity he would like to do at that time. Direct him to continue in the same manner to complete the remaining sections of his paper with an afternoon and then an evening time and activity. After students label their drawings, encourage each child to share his schedule while modeling the named times on a demonstration clock.

eat chocolate doughnuts
8:00

swim
12:00

7:00
read books

Find reproducible activities on pages 48–49.

TEC60983

TEC60983

TEC60983

TEC60983

This Year Has Been a Treat!

Name _____

My Friends

My "Berry" Favorite Subject

A Book Ripe for Reading

My Sweet Teacher

A Refreshing Memory

A Taste of Summer

Name _____

Write each group of words in ABC order.

ice

cup   sweet
yellow   lemon

1. _____
2. _____
3. _____
4. _____
5. _____

sip

red   berry
cool   yummy

1. _____
2. _____
3. _____
4. _____
5. _____

cold

dish   spoon
treat   good

1. _____
2. _____
3. _____
4. _____
5. _____

dessert

cherry   melt
stem   lick

1. _____
2. _____
3. _____
4. _____
5. _____

Arts & Crafts

Butterfly Garden

Painted pasta makes for a unique way to showcase butterflies in all stages of development! Use a small paintbrush and tempera paints to decorate bow-tie pasta (butterflies), spiral pasta (caterpillars), and small shell pasta (chrysalides). While the paint is drying, use watercolors to paint a garden scene on a sheet of white construction paper. After the paint is dry, glue the pasta to the scene and draw clusters of small butterfly eggs on plant leaves.

Beautiful Bouquet

To make a flower, cut evenly spaced slits from the rim to the bottom of a three-ounce paper cup. Gently flatten the cup to spread out the resulting petals. Make two other flowers in the same manner, varying the widths of the petals. Paint the undecorated sides of the flowers and allow time for them to dry. Then tape a green pipe cleaner to the back of each flower to resemble a stem. Tie the stems together with ribbon to create a vibrant bouquet!

A Berry for Mom

This personalized note holder is not only pleasing to look at but it smells great too! Mix one envelope of unsweetened, strawberry-flavored drink mix with two tablespoons of white glue. To make a strawberry note holder, paint a jumbo macaroni shell with the glue mixture. While the glue is still wet, attach green tissue paper leaves and sprinkle red glitter on the shell. After the shell is dry, hot glue (for teacher use only) it to a wooden spring-type clothespin. Next, attach a strip of magnetic tape to the back of the clothespin. Complete a tagboard copy of one of the Mother's Day cards on page 53, and clip it to the note holder.

Dear Mama,

You are sweet like a strawberry;
Yes, it's true!
Here are some reasons
Why I love you:

You give me hugs.

You read me books.

You tuck me in.

Love,

Carter

Uninvited Guests

Ants are marching all over this picnic-themed placemat! To make a placemat, fold a 9" x 12" sheet of red construction paper in half lengthwise. Starting at the fold, cut slits in the paper at one-inch intervals as shown. Open the paper and weave 1" x 12" white construction paper strips through the slits. Glue the ends of the strips in place. Dip a pencil eraser or cotton swab in black paint and make sets of three dots to resemble ants. After the paint is dry, use a fine-tip marker to add six legs and antennae to each ant.

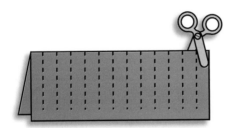

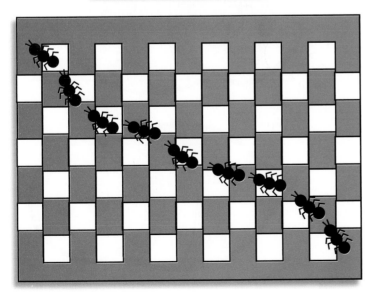

Busy Beehive

To make a beehive, position a large foam cup upside down and paint it with diluted glue. Place a natural (brown) coffee filter over the top and secure it to the glue. Cut out and discard the centers from two additional coffee filters. Use the resulting pleats to cover the remainder of the cup. Cut out a yellow construction paper copy of the bee patterns at the bottom of this page. For each bee, form wings from a small piece of clear plastic wrap. Glue the wings to the bees. Tape each bee to a four-inch spiraled piece of pipe cleaner. Poke the free end of each pipe cleaner into the beehive to resemble bees buzzing around a hive.

Bee Patterns
Use with "It's a Date!" on page 32 and with "Busy Beehive" on this page.

Dear _____,

You are sweet like a strawberry;

Yes, it's true!

Here are some reasons

Why I love you:

_____

_____

_____

Love,

_____

©The Mailbox® • *Organize May Now!*™ • TEC60983

Have a "Berry" Happy Mother's Day!

Glue photo here.

Love,

_____

©The Mailbox® • *Organize May Now!*™ • TEC60983

Recognize youngsters' hard work with this springtime display! Mount student-made construction paper flowers on a board decorated like the one shown. Invite each youngster to choose a favorite piece of work and display it above the garden. Periodically ask youngsters to choose a more current work sample to update the display.

In advance, obtain a small school photo of each child. Invite students to share what they have learned during this school year. Write their responses on a beehive-shaped piece of bulletin board paper. Have each youngster cut out a yellow construction paper copy of the bee pattern on page 56. Ask him to draw black stripes on the bee's body and then glue on pipe cleaner antennae and waxed paper wings. Then direct him to glue his photo to his bee. Display the bees and beehive along with the title shown.

Displays

For this end-of-the-year display, have each youngster personalize a baseball cutout (patterns on page 61). Then direct her to draw or write about a favorite memory from the past school year on a sheet of paper. Mount the completed papers with their corresponding balls. Add a title similar to the one shown.

Invite your soon-to-be-graduates to think about the upcoming school year. Have each child cut out a construction paper copy of the butterfly pattern on page 57. Direct her to write on her butterfly about a goal she has for the next school year. Then invite each youngster to use art materials to add antennae and decorate her butterfly as desired. Mount the finished projects and the title as shown.

Bee Pattern

Use with "Bee Buddies" on page 32 and "'Un-bee-lievable' Kids!" on page 54.

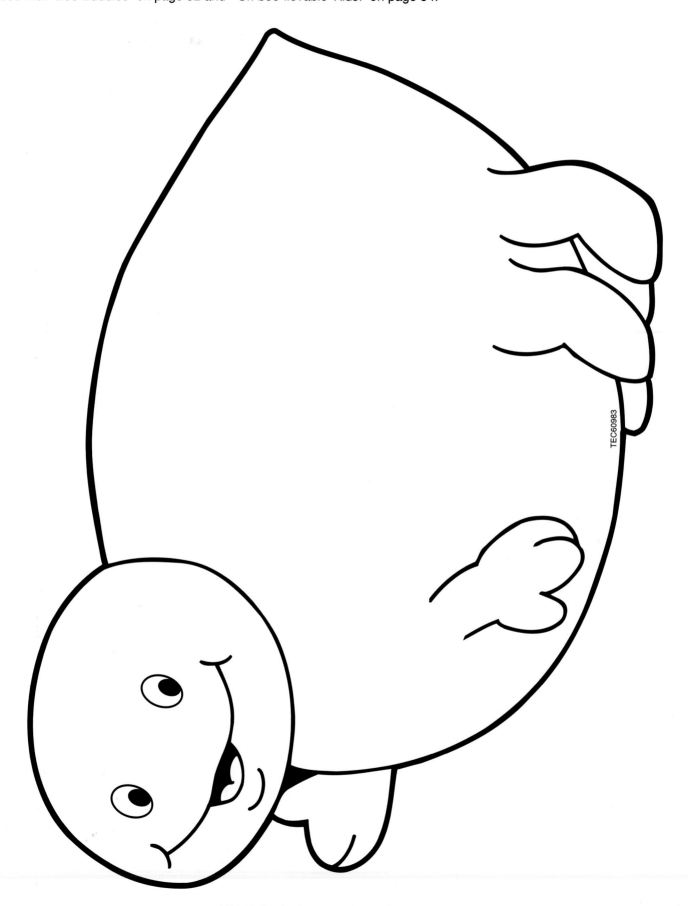

TEC60983

Centers

Math

Patterns

Ant Parade

To prepare for this partner center, cut out three construction paper copies of the ant cards on page 60. Store the cards in a picnic basket (or other similar container) along with a tablecloth. Place the basket at a center. When a twosome visits the center, they spread out the tablecloth. One player uses the cards to make an ant pattern on the tablecloth. Then the other student extends it. After checking the pattern, players return the cards to the basket and switch roles.

Onsets and rimes

Literacy

Two in a Pot

Real and nonsense words are sure to bloom at this word-formation center! Program a small white flower cutout for each rime that you would like youngsters to practice. Label a supply of small colorful flower cutouts each with a different onset. Glue each flower to a craft stick. Press a mound of clay in the bottom of a plastic flowerpot or small cup. Place the pot, the flowers, and a supply of lined paper at a center.

A child inserts a colorful flower and white flower in the pot so that they are held upright by the clay. She decides whether the flowers form a real or nonsense word and writes the word on her paper. If it is a real word, she draws a check next to it. If it is a nonsense word, she draws an *X* next to it. Leaving the rime in place, she continues in the same manner for each remaining colorful flower. Then she repeats the activity with a different white flower.

Play Ball!

Use the pattern on page 61 to make a supply of construction paper bats. Program each bat with a different unpunctuated sentence, including questions, statements, and exclamations. Also cut out a copy of the baseballs on page 61 and program each ball with a different ending punctuation mark. If desired, store the balls in a mitt. Place the balls and the bats at a center stocked with paper. A youngster takes a bat and reads the sentence. After she uses a ball to correctly punctuate it, she writes the sentence on her paper. Then she repeats the activity by going to bat again!

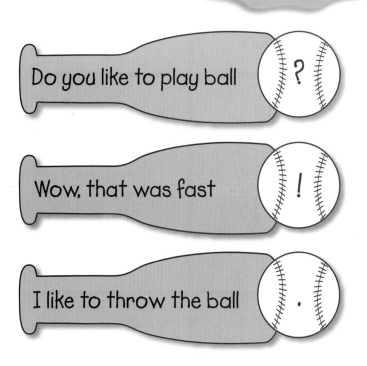

Do you like to play ball ?

Wow, that was fast !

I like to throw the ball .

Build a Sun

On each of two yellow construction paper circles (suns), draw a happy face and write a different number from 4–7. For each sun, program orange triangles (sun rays) with corresponding addition and subtraction facts. If desired, program the backs of the cutouts for self-checking. Store the cutouts in a large resealable plastic bag. Then place the bag at a center along with a pair of sunglasses. A student dons the glasses and assembles the suns.

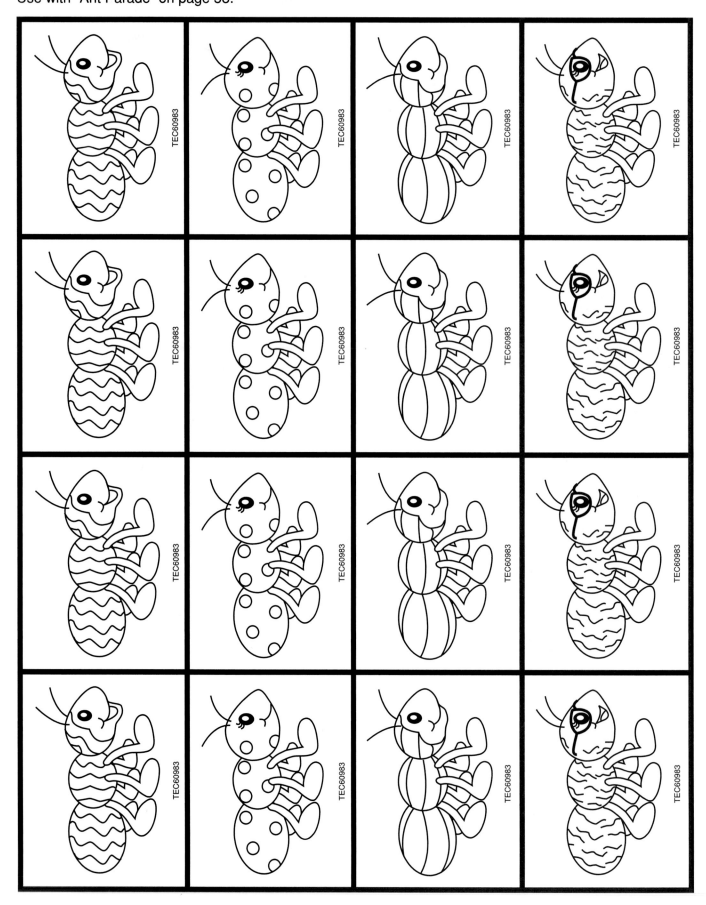

Use with "Kindergarten Was…a Ball!" on page 55 and "Play Ball!" on page 59.

TEC60983

TEC60983

TEC60983

TEC60983

Games

Skill review

Buzz!

To prepare for this phonics review, make several yellow construction paper copies of the bee cards on page 64. Cut out the cards and program each one to reinforce a chosen type of phonetic element, such as initial consonants, blends, or digraphs. Have students sit in a circle. Hand a few students the prepared cards. To begin, buzz like a bee as students pass the cards around the group. Stop buzzing after a few moments. At this signal, have the youngsters stop passing the bee cards. Go around the group, asking each student holding a card to say the corresponding sound and to name a word with the phonetic element. Resume the buzzing to continue the activity.

Comparing sets

Math

Flower Bug

Reinforce sorting and counting skills with this colorful activity. Gather 15 artificial flowers or flower cutouts in two different colors and place them in a plastic vase or other similar container. Also make a bug headband by attaching two pipe cleaner antennae to a paper strip and securing the strip's ends in place to fit a child's head. Choose one child to be the bug and wear the headband. Choose ten other students to each pick a flower. Play some lively music as the students sort themselves by flower color and as the bug flies around. When the flowers are sorted, direct the bug to count aloud the number of flowers in each group. Challenge the remaining students to announce which group of flowers has more and which group has less. Then have youngsters return the flowers to the vase and play again with different students.

Fractions: parts of a group

Shark!

For this small-group activity, program separate blank cards with the fractions ¼, ½, ¾, ⅓, and ⅔. Place the fraction cards in a container along with a copy of the shark card on page 65. Also make enough copies of the fish cards on page 65 for each child to have one card.

To play, give each child a fish card. Draw one card from the container and show it to the students. If it is a fraction card, each child determines whether she has the matching fish group on her card. If so, she holds up her card as she says the corresponding fraction. If a shark card is drawn, all students stand up and announce, "Shark!" Then each child exchanges cards with a neighbor and sits down.

Following oral directions

Packing for a Picnic

Reinforce two- and three-step directions with a small-group activity that has youngsters packing picnic supplies. Gather a variety of picnic-related items, such as plastic food, napkins, paper plates, cups, plastic forks, and a checkered tablecloth. Place the items beside a picnic basket or cooler. To play, choose a youngster to be the "picnic packer." Have the youngster follow a two- or three-step set of directions related to packing for a picnic. Consider directions such as "Pack three plates and four napkins" or "Pack one apple, three cups, and five plates." After verifying the supplies, unpack the basket and play again.

Bee Cards ● ● ● ● ● ● ● ● ● ● ● ● ● ● ● ● ●
Use with "Buzz!" on page 62.

TEC60983

TEC60983

TEC60983

TEC60983

TEC60983

TEC60983

TEC60983

TEC60983

TEC60983

Games 65

Management Tips

Seeing Spots

It's easy to spot good behavior with this cute-as-a-bug incentive! For each child, personalize a white construction paper copy of the ladybug pattern on page 67. Have her color and cut out her bug and then glue on six construction paper legs. When the critters are dry, display them on a board titled "Spot Our Good Behavior." Each time a student exhibits good behavior, invite her to attach a black paper circle to her bug. At the end of the week, reward students who have collected a predetermined number of ladybug spots. Then remove the spots and repeat the process the following week.

Bag It

Add seasonal flair to your desktop and end clutter with this spiffy idea. Select a gift bag with a holiday or seasonal design. Place the bag on your desk and use it to store seasonal stickers, notepads, name tags, and awards. Not only will your desk be organized but you'll have an easy-to-carry collection of supplies!

Thanks, Volunteers!

This flowery thank-you gift is sure to bring smiles to your classroom volunteers! To make the vase, cut off the bottom section of a two-liter bottle for each volunteer you would like to recognize. Then have each child use a colored permanent marker to sign his name on each vase. To make the flowers for several vases, have each youngster paint a large craft stick green for a stem. When the paint is dry, help him write a kind word or short phrase on his stem. Then have him cut out a construction paper flower and glue it on the stem. After the flowers dry, press a layer of clay into the bottom of each vase and insert several flowers. Finally, fill each vase with colorful paper shreds.

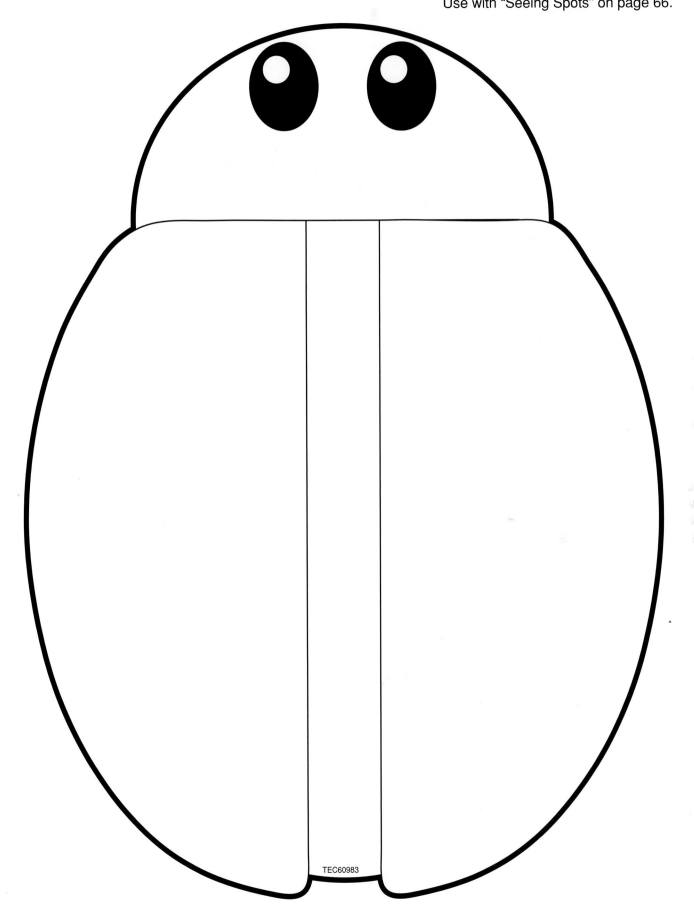

TEC60983

Good Guess!

Improve critical-thinking skills with this five-minute filler. Program a supply of blank cards, each with a set of three related seasonal words. For example, a card could be labeled "petals, stem, leaves" *(parts of a flower)* or "Mother's Day, Memorial Day, Cinco de Mayo" *(May holidays).* Place the cards in a decorated gift bag. When you have a few minutes to spare, invite a student to choose a card. Have him read the three words aloud and guess how the words are related. If needed, encourage him to ask a classmate for assistance.

lamb

chick

bunny

These are all baby animals.

Growing Spellers

Youngsters grow to enjoy spelling practice when they gather around for this quick activity. Ask students to squat and pretend to be seeds planted in the ground. Announce a spelling word. Then encourage students to slowly stretch upward—like a flower growing toward the sun—as they slowly spell the word aloud. After verifying the correct spelling, direct youngsters to squat back down. Then repeat the activity with additional words.

S-P-R-I-N-G!

Editor's Buzz

When you have a few extra minutes, write two seasonal words on the board and ask a child to read the words aloud. Invite her to create a sentence that includes the two words. As she dictates her sentence, write it on the board with several mistakes for student editing. Then ask a different student to edit the sentence on the board. Finally, help the class check the sentence and add any additional editing marks.

bee   flower

the bee flew to the flower.

Ice-Cream Dream

Reinforce rhyming skills with this mouthwatering time filler. Tell youngsters that some ice-cream flavors have rhyming names, such as Ben & Jerry's Chubby Hubby or Chunky Monkey. Encourage each child to dream up a new ice-cream flavor with an original rhyming name. Then invite youngsters to share their new flavors and, if desired, their ingredients.

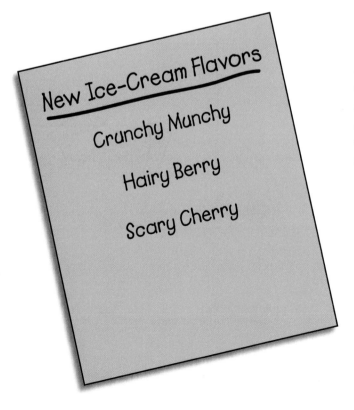

New Ice-Cream Flavors

Crunchy Munchy

Hairy Berry

Scary Cherry

Journal Prompts

- Write about a new friend you met this school year.

- You've just found a juicy, ripe strawberry. Write about where you found it and what you will do with it.

- If you could fly like a bee, where would you go? What would you do?

- Mother's Day is in May. What makes a mom a really great mom?

- Pretend you're an earthworm. Then write about a warm, sunny day in the flower garden.

- Would a ladybug be the same if it had stripes instead of spots? Why or why not?

- If you could visit anyone in the world this summer, who would it be? Why?

- What is the best way to catch a fish?

Use one or more of the following ideas and the fish pattern on page 72 to get your youngsters hooked on writing.

- Give each child a copy of the pattern and have her decorate it with a variety of craft supplies. Then, on a separate sheet of paper, have her describe her fish. Gather students in a circle and scatter the fish in the middle. Read each description and invite students to determine which fish is being described.

- Use the fish pattern for journal writing. Write the last prompt from above on a copy of the pattern, adding writing lines if desired; then make a class supply.

- Give each child a copy of the fish pattern and have him write about his favorite memory of the school year. Then display the completed fish with the title "Our School is Cool!" Encourage students to read the fish for a swim down memory lane.

Crystal
My fish is sparkly. It has pink fins and a blue mouth.

Flower Power

Start this activity with a graphic organizer and watch youngsters' writing skills bloom! Write a story idea (see suggestions) on a copy of page 73 and make student copies. Have each child plan her story by answering each question in detail. Then direct her to use her completed organizer to write a story. In no time, you'll have a bouquet of fresh writing!

Story Ideas
The Sunflower That Does Not Like the Sun
The Mysterious Plant in the Garden
The Singing Flower

Posy Planner

Name Hollyn

Story idea:

The Singing Flower

What happens first?

A boy waters the flower with lemonade.

What happens next?

The flower starts to sing. The boy takes him to a singing contest.

What happens last?

The flower wins first place.

Wish You Were Here!

Ask each child to imagine himself vacationing in an exciting place. Invite him to consider what important details he'd like to share with a friend. Then have him write a postcard-style message to the friend on one side of a lined 5" x 7" index card. Have each child draw a scene from his vacation on the back of the card. Encourage students to include themselves in their illustrations. Bind the completed postcards into a class book titled "Vacation Greetings!"

Dear Brock,
I'm at the beach. I went surfing yesterday. Wish you were here!

Your friend,
Steve

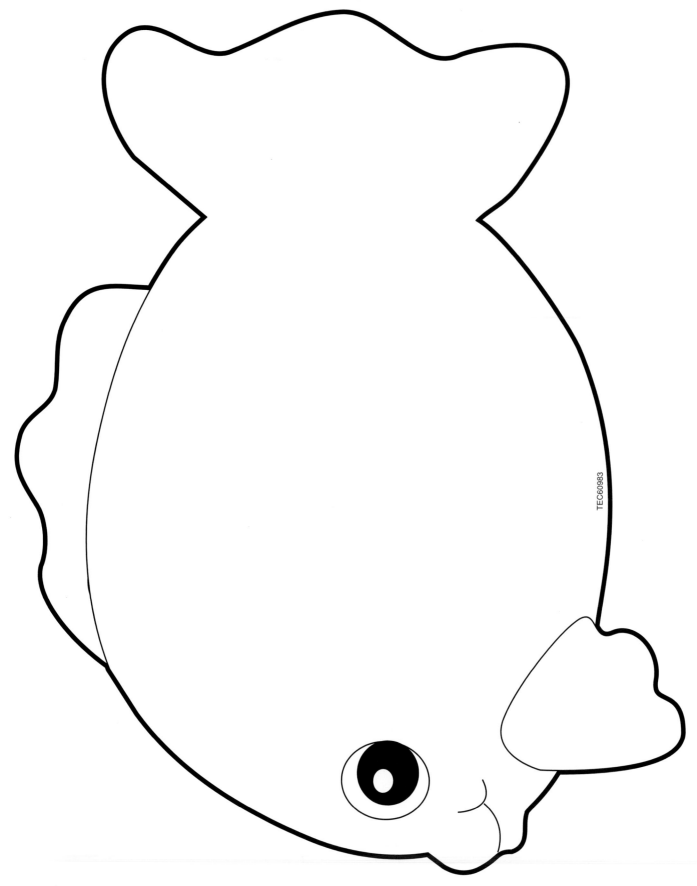

TEC60983

Posy Planner

Name _____

Story idea:

What happens first?

What happens next?

What happens last?

Note to the teacher: Use with "Flower Power" on page 71.

A Box of Blooms

A ready-to-use center mat and cards for two different learning levels

Materials:

center mat to the right
center cards on page 77 (easier reading level)
center cards on page 79 (more challenging
    reading level)
2 resealable plastic bags

Preparing the center:

Cut out the cards and place each set in a
separate bag.

Using the center:

1. A child removes the cards from one bag and
   lays them faceup in the center area.
2. She chooses a sentence card and places it on
   the mat.
3. She reads the sentence and then places the corresponding punctuation card on the mat.
4. To check her work, she flips over the sentence card.
   If the answer matches, she places the sentence card
   in the bag. If it does not, she rereads the sentence
   and chooses the correct punctuation mark; then she
   places the sentence card in the bag.
5. She repeats Steps 2 through 4 for each remaining
   sentence card.

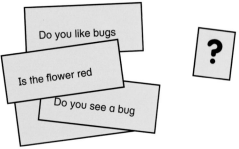

Follow-Up

After a child completes the center
activity, use the skill sheet on page
81 for more practice.

A Box of Blooms

Put a sentence card on the box.
Read.
Put the punctuation card on the box.
Check.

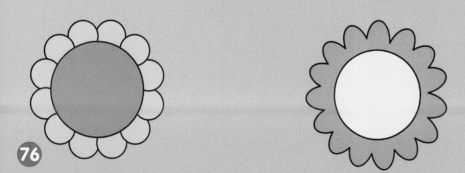

The flowers need water

The flowers need sun

The flowers are tall

The box is big

Do you see a bug

How tall are the flowers

Is the flower red

Do you like bugs

.

?

A Box of Blooms
TEC60983

A Box of Blooms
TEC60983

A Box of Blooms
TEC60983

A Box of Blooms
TEC60983

A Box of Blooms
TEC60983

A Box of Blooms
TEC60983

A Box of Blooms
TEC60983

A Box of Blooms
TEC60983

A Box of Blooms
TEC60983

A Box of Blooms
TEC60983

Center Cards

Use with the directions on page 74.

There are four flowers in the box	The big flower smells the best
The flower box is big and yelllow	The red flower is very tall
Do you like purple flowers	How many flowers do you see
Have you seen the pretty flowers	Does the bug like the flowers
	.
	?

A Box of Blooms
TEC60983

A Box of Blooms
TEC60983

A Box of Blooms
TEC60983

A Box of Blooms
TEC60983

A Box of Blooms
TEC60983

A Box of Blooms
TEC60983

A Box of Blooms
TEC60983

A Box of Blooms
TEC60983

A Box of Blooms
TEC60983

Totally Tulips

Name _____

Write a **.** or **?** in each box.
Color the flowers by the code.

Color Code

. — red
? — blue

There should be five flowers of each color.

1 Do you like flowers ☐

2 I like to plant flowers ☐

3 The red flower smells nice ☐

4 The purple one is pretty ☐

5 Do you want to smell it ☐

6 I see three flowers in the box ☐

7 Do you see any bugs ☐

8 Which flower is the biggest ☐

9 Is that flower the smallest ☐

10 I will water the flowers ☐

Biscuits and Honey

A ready-to-use center mat and cards for two different learning levels

Materials:

center mat to the right
center cards on page 85 (addition to 10 with manipulatives)
center cards on page 87 (addition to 18)
blank paper
2 resealable plastic bags

Preparing the center:

Cut out the cards and place each set in a separate bag.

Using the center:

1. A child removes the cards from a bag and lays them faceup in the center area.
2. **For addition to 10,** he chooses a word problem card and places it on the mat. He solves the problem, using the manipulatives. Then he places the corresponding answer card on the mat. **For addition to 18,** he chooses a problem card and places it on the mat. He writes and solves the math sentence on a sheet of paper; then he places the corresponding answer card on the mat.
3. To check his work, he flips over the cards. If the backs of the cards match, he places the cards back in the bag. If they do not match, he reworks the problem. Then he finds the correct answer card and places both cards in the bag.

Biscuits and Honey

Put.
Solve.
Check.

3 bees eat.
3 more bees eat.
How many bees eat in all?

HONEY

6

Follow-Up

After a child completes the center activity for addition to 10, use the skill sheet on page 89 for more practice.

Biscuits and Honey

Put.

Solve.

Check.

Center Cards

Use with the directions on page 82.

There are 2 big bees. There are 3 small bees. How many bees are there in all?	3 bees eat. 3 more bees eat. How many bees eat in all?
2 bees work. 2 more bees work. How many bees work in all?	7 bees fly. 2 more bees fly. How many bees fly in all?
5 bees buzz. 3 more bees buzz. How many bees buzz in all?	6 bees dance. 4 more bees dance. How many bees dance in all?

5	6
4	9
8	10

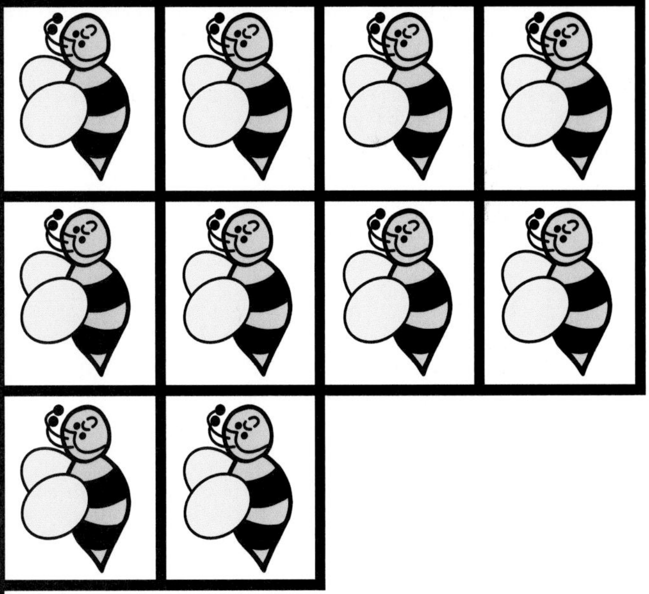

Biscuits and Honey
TEC60983

Biscuits and Honey
TEC60983

Biscuits and Honey
TEC60983

Biscuits and Honey
TEC60983

Biscuits and Honey
TEC60983

Biscuits and Honey
TEC60983

Biscuits and Honey
TEC60983

Biscuits and Honey
TEC60983

Biscuits and Honey
TEC60983

Biscuits and Honey
TEC60983

Biscuits and Honey
TEC60983

Biscuits and Honey
TEC60983

Biscuits and Honey
TEC60983

Biscuits and Honey
TEC60983

Biscuits and Honey
TEC60983

Biscuits and Honey
TEC60983

Biscuits and Honey
TEC60983

Biscuits and Honey
TEC60983

Biscuits and Honey
TEC60983

Biscuits and Honey
TEC60983

Biscuits and Honey
TEC60983

Biscuits and Honey
TEC60983

There are 6 hot biscuits.
There are 7 cool biscuits.
How many biscuits are there in all?

7 bees stop to eat.
9 more bees join in.
How many bees eat in all?

8 bees fly by.
6 more bees fly by.
How many bees fly by in all?

9 bees buzz.
9 more bees buzz.
How many bees buzz in all?

The bees eat 7 biscuits.
They eat 8 more biscuits.
How many biscuits do they eat in all?

There are 6 big jars of honey.
There are 6 small jars of honey.
How many jars in all?

8 bees nap.
9 more bees nap.
How many bees nap in all?

6 bees land on grass.
5 bees land on flowers.
How many bees land in all?

| 11 | 12 | 13 | 14 |
| 15 | 16 | 17 | 18 |

Biscuits and Honey
TEC60983

Biscuits and Honey
TEC60983

Biscuits and Honey
TEC60983

Biscuits and Honey
TEC60983

Biscuits and Honey
TEC60983

Biscuits and Honey
TEC60983

Biscuits and Honey
TEC60983

Biscuits and Honey
TEC60983

Biscuits and Honey
TEC60983

Biscuits and Honey
TEC60983

Biscuits and Honey
TEC60983

Biscuits and Honey
TEC60983

Biscuits and Honey
TEC60983

Biscuits and Honey
TEC60983

Biscuits and Honey
TEC60983

Biscuits and Honey
TEC60983

Buzzin' Around

Name _____

Read.
Write the math sentence.
Use the counters to help you.

3 bees buzz. 3 more bees buzz. How many bees buzz in all? _____ + _____ = _____ bees	5 bees fly. 3 more bees fly. How many bees fly in all? _____ + _____ = _____ bees
2 bees eat honey. 2 more bees eat honey. How many bees eat honey in all? _____ + _____ = _____ bees	I bee naps. 4 more bees nap. How many bees nap in all? _____ + _____ = _____ bees
4 bees are on the flower. 5 more bees join them. How many bees are on the flower in all? _____ + _____ = _____ bees	3 bees land. 7 more bees land. How many bees land in all? _____ + _____ = _____ bees

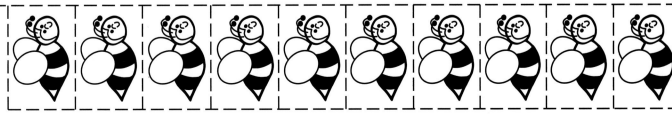

Beach Towel Pals

Name _____

Glue to match the pictures and the beginning letters.

Bb

Tt

Initial Consonants: b, t

Beach Patrol

Name _____

✂ Cut.

Glue in order.

LIFEGUARD ON DUTY

©The Mailbox® • *Organize May Now!*™ • TEC60983

Friday	Monday	Saturday	Tuesday
Thursday	Wednesday	Sunday	

Lounging Ladybugs

Name _____

Cut. Glue to match the word family. Write each word.

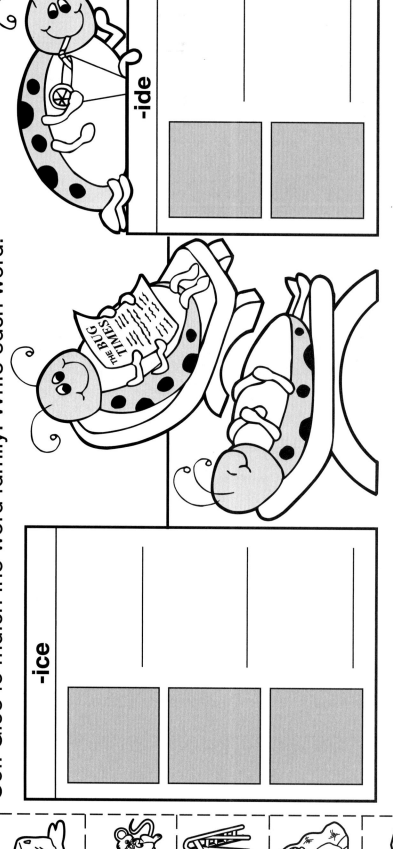

-ide

-ice

Complete each sentence with a word from above.

1. The _____ wore a white wedding gown.

2. The _____ have long tails.

3. Roll the two _____ .

4. The _____ melts when it is hot outside.

Long-Vowel Word Families: *-ice, -ide*

Batter Up!

Name _____

Cut. Glue to match the contractions.

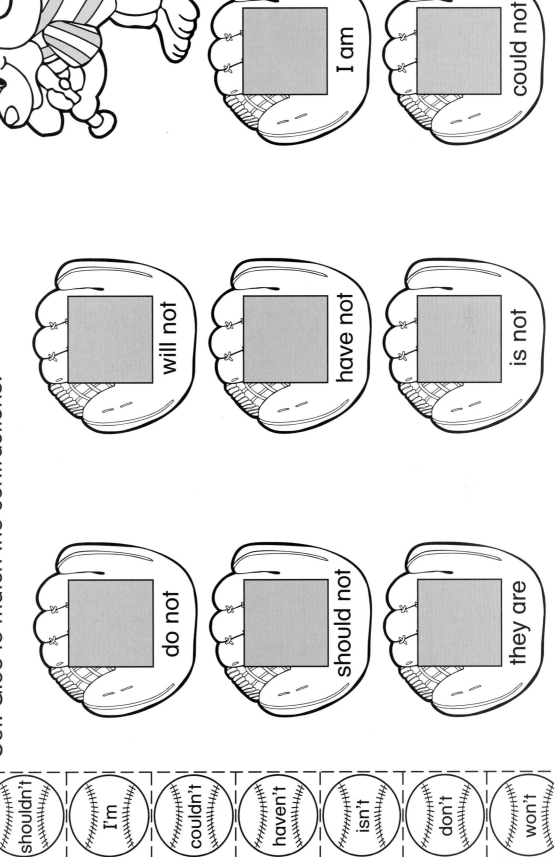

I am

could not

will not

have not

is not

do not

should not

they are

they're

shouldn't

I'm

couldn't

haven't

isn't

don't

won't

Wingspan

Name _____

✂ Cut. Measure. ✏ Write the length.

Nonstandard Measurement

Dairy Delight

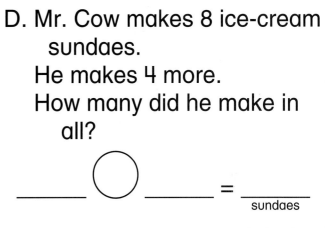

Name _____

Read.
Decide if you must add or subtract.
Write the math sentence.

A. There are 9 nuts on the sundae.
Mr. Cow adds 7 nuts.
How many nuts in all?

_____ ◯ _____ = _____
nuts

D. Mr. Cow makes 8 ice-cream sundaes.
He makes 4 more.
How many did he make in all?

_____ ◯ _____ = _____
sundaes

B. Mr. Cow sells 6 ice-cream cones.
He sells 7 more.
How many does he sell in all?

_____ ◯ _____ = _____
ice-cream cones

E. Mr. Cow makes a sundae with 14 cherries.
8 cherries fall off.
How many are left?

_____ ◯ _____ = _____
cherries

C. Mr. Cow makes 12 milk shakes.
He sells 9.
How many are left?

_____ ◯ _____ = _____
milk shakes

F. Mr. Cow has 17 tubs of ice cream.
He uses 9 tubs.
How many are left?

_____ ◯ _____ = _____
tubs

Grand Flower Stand

Name _____

Add or subtract.

Color each flower by the code.

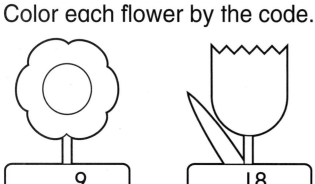

Flower Sale!

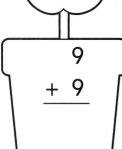

9
+ 9

18
− 9

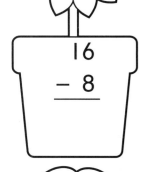

16
− 8

7
+ 5

8
+ 6

17
− 8

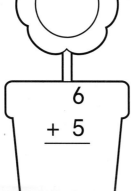

14
− 7

6
+ 5

8
+ 9

9
+ 6